Rosa Parks

Terry Barber

ACTIVIST SERIES

Rosa Parks is published by
Grass Roots Press, a division of Literacy Services of Canada Ltd.

PHONE 1–888–303–3213
WEBSITE www.grassrootsbooks.net

ACKNOWLEDGEMENTS

We acknowledge the financial support of the Government of Canada through the
Book Publishing Industry Development Program (BPIDP) for our publishing activities.

We acknowledge the support of
the Alberta Foundation for the Arts
for our publishing programs.

Editor: Dr. Pat Campbell
Image Research: Dr. Pat Campbell
Book design: Lara Minja, Lime Design Inc.

Library and Archives Canada Cataloguing in Publication

Barber, Terry, date
    Rosa Parks / Terry Barber.

(Activist series)
ISBN 978–1–894593–44–1

    1. Parks, Rosa, 1913–. 2. African Americans—Alabama—
Montgomery—Biography. 3. Civil rights workers—Alabama—
Montgomery—Biography. 4. Readers for new literates. I. Title.
II. Series.

F334.M753P37 2006   428.6'2   C2006–900420–X

Printed in Canada

Contents

Early Years 5

December 1, 1955 13

Rosa is Arrested 17

The Montgomery Bus Boycott 23

The U.S. Supreme Court Ruling 35

After the Bus Boycott 37

Glossary 46

Talking About the Book 47

Rosa as a baby.

Early Years

It is 1913. A black baby girl is born.
One day, she will change history.
Her name is Rosa. She is the first child
of James and Leona McCauley.

Rosa and her family live on a farm in Pine Level.

Early Years

Rosa's mother teaches school. Rosa's father is a carpenter. When Rosa is two, her father goes north to find work. Rosa moves to Pine Level, Alabama, with her mother and baby brother. Rosa's family lives with her grandparents.

This is a one-room school for black children.

Early Years

Rosa goes to an all-black school. It is a one-room school. White children go to a bigger school. White children get a better education.

Rosa sews at work.

Early Years

Rosa marries Raymond Parks in 1932. Raymond is a barber. Rosa is a **seamstress.** They live in Montgomery, Alabama.

Rosa gets her high school diploma in 1934.

Rosa Parks gets on the bus.

December 1, 1955

Rosa Parks takes a bus home from work. The bus is full. The black people are sitting. Some white people are standing.

Rosa Parks sits in the bus.

December 1, 1955

The bus driver tells the black people to give up their seats. Three blacks give up their seats. Rosa Parks will not give up her seat. She is fed up. She does not want to be a second-class citizen. She wants the same rights as white people.

"Are you going to stand up?" the bus driver asks.

"No," Rosa Parks says.

"Well, by God, I am going to have you arrested," the bus driver says.

"You may do that," Rosa Parks says.

Rosa and her lawyer go to court.

Rosa is Arrested

The police come and arrest Rosa Parks. She is put in jail for a few hours. She is charged with breaking **Jim Crow laws.** Four days later, Rosa Parks goes to court. The judge says, "You are guilty." She gets a $10 fine.

Jim Crow Laws

These laws segregate black and white people. They cannot go to the same school. They cannot use the same water fountain.

18

Rosa is Arrested

The Jim Crow laws keep black and white people apart. Black people must sit in the back of the bus. White people get to sit in the front. These laws support **segregation.**

Public places are segregated.

Rosa is Arrested

News of Rosa Parks' arrest spreads.
Black people in Montgomery are fed up.
Segregation is wrong. Jim Crow laws
are wrong. Black people want laws
that support equal rights.

People meet to talk about the boycott.

The Montgomery Bus Boycott

Rosa Parks' brave act starts a bus **boycott** in Montgomery. Black leaders ask all black people to stop riding the buses. The boycott is a way to say segregation is wrong.

Martin Luther King Jr. gives a speech.

The Montgomery Bus Boycott

Martin Luther King Jr. is a preacher.
He becomes the leader of the bus
boycott. He gives speeches. The
speeches give people hope. He tells the
black people to **unite.** Martin Luther
King Jr. wants to end segregation.
He wants equal rights.

These people walk during the bus boycott.

The Montgomery Bus Boycott

Black people stop riding the buses. Some black people ride in **car pools.** Others ride in cabs. Most black people walk. Some must walk miles and miles. The bus company loses money.

The bus company loses 65% of its business.

The police charge these three men.

The Montgomery Bus Boycott

White people want the buses to
run again. They say the bus boycott
is not legal. The police charge 90
black people for taking part in the
bus boycott.

The Montgomery Bus Boycott

The police arrest Rosa Parks again.
The police take her fingerprints.
The police take her mug shot.

People do not ride the buses.

The Montgomery Bus Boycott

Many black people lose their jobs.
Rosa Parks loses her job as a
seamstress. She gets death threats.
But black people will not ride the
buses. They do not ride the buses
for 381 days.

Martin Luther King Jr. sits beside a white man.

The U.S. Supreme Court Ruling

In late 1956, the U.S. Supreme Court makes a ruling. The court rules that segregation on buses is wrong. Black people start riding the buses again. Black people can choose where to sit. Black people do not have to give up their seats to whites.

Rosa walks in a protest.

After the
Bus Boycott

Rosa Parks cannot find work. She
leaves Montgomery. In 1957, she
moves to Detroit with her husband
and mother. In time, Rosa builds a
better life in Detroit. Her fame grows.
Rosa Parks keeps working in the civil
rights movement.

Rosa stands beside Bill Clinton.
She wears the Medal of Freedom.

After the Bus Boycott

Rosa Parks gets many honours. Two
cities name streets after her. A museum
and a library are built in her honour.
President Clinton gives her the Medal
of Freedom.

Oprah Winfrey speaks at Rosa's funeral.

After the Bus Boycott

Rosa Parks dies on October 24, 2005.
She dies of natural causes. She is 92
years old. Many famous people go
to her funeral. People remember her
as the Mother of the civil rights
movement.

This is Rosa at her home in 1988.

After the Bus Boycott

People remember Rosa Parks as a
special person. She believed in
freedom. She believed in equal rights.
Fame did not change Rosa Parks.
She treated all people with respect.

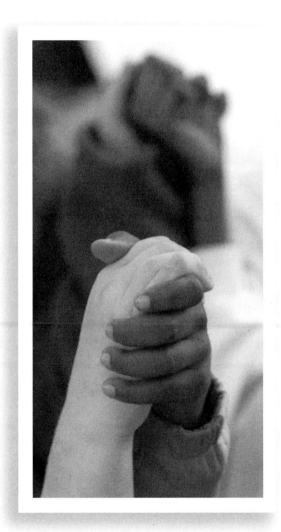

These children honour the
50th anniversary of the
Montgomery bus boycott.

After the Bus Boycott

Rosa Parks' brave act changed history on December 1, 1955. This shows how one person can change the world. We all leave paths that others can follow. Rosa Parks' courage has made the world a better place.

Glossary

boycott: to refuse to use a service or buy a product.

car pool: a group of people who ride together in one car.

seamstress: a woman who sews for a living.

segregation: the act of separating a race or class from the rest of society.

unite: to bring or join together.

Jim Crow laws: these laws made segregation a legal act. For example, black and white people could not use the same waiting room, entrance, school, or water fountain.

Talking About the Book

What did you learn about Rosa Parks?

What did you learn about the
Montgomery bus boycott?

What words would you use to describe
Rosa Parks?

Why do you think Rosa Parks is called
the Mother of the civil rights movement?

How do you think Rosa Parks has made
the world a better place?

Picture Credits